D1611890

save the . . .
ELEPHANTS

by **Sarah L. Thomson**
with an introduction
by **Chelsea Clinton**

PHILOMEL

PHILOMEL BOOKS
An imprint of Penguin Random House LLC, New York

First published in the United States of America by Philomel Books,
an imprint of Penguin Random House LLC, 2022

Text copyright © 2022 by Chelsea Clinton

Philomel Books is a registered trademark of Penguin Random House LLC.

Visit us online at penguinrandomhouse.com.

Library of Congress Cataloging-in-Publication Data is available.

Printed in the United States of America

ISBN 9780593404232 (hardcover)
ISBN 9780593404249 (paperback)

10 9 8 7 6 5 4 3 2 1

WOR

Edited by Jill Santopolo and Talia Benamy
Design by Lily Qian
Text set in Calisto MT Pro

save the . . .

save the . . .
BLUE WHALES

save the . . .
ELEPHANTS

save the . . .
FROGS

save the . . .
GIRAFFES

save the . . .
GORILLAS

save the . . .
LIONS

save the . . .
POLAR BEARS

save the . . .
TIGERS

save the . . .
WHALE SHARKS

Dear Reader,

When I was around your age, my favorite animals were dinosaurs and elephants. I wanted to know everything I could about triceratopses, stegosauruses and other dinosaurs that had roamed our earth millions of years ago. Elephants, though, captured my curiosity and my heart. The more I learned about the largest animals on land today, the more I wanted to do to help keep them and other endangered species safe forever.

So I joined organizations working around the world to support endangered species and went to our local zoo to learn more about conservation efforts close to home (thanks to my parents and grandparents). I tried to learn as much as I could about how we can ensure animals and plants don't go extinct like the dinosaurs, especially since it's the choices that we're making that pose the greatest threat to their lives today.

The choices we make don't have to be huge to make

a real difference. When I was in elementary school, I used to cut up the plastic rings around six-packs of soda, glue them to brightly colored construction paper (purple was my favorite) and hand them out to whomever would take one in a one-girl campaign to raise awareness about the dangers that plastic six-pack rings posed to marine wildlife around the world. I learned about that from a book—*50 Simple Things Kids Can Do to Save the Earth*—which helped me understand that you're never too young to make a difference and that we all can change the world. I hope that this book will inform and inspire you to help save this and other endangered species. There are tens of thousands of species that are currently under threat, with more added every year. We have the power to save those species, and with your help, we can.

Sincerely,

Chelsea Clinton

save the . . .
ELEPHANTS

CONTENTS

1

JUNGLES, GRASSLANDS, AND TEMPLES: WHERE ELEPHANTS LIVE

An elephant isn't hard to spot. It's the biggest animal that lives on land. If you're going to look for one, you'd better head to the grasslands or forests of Africa or to the jungles of Southeast Asia. You'll find a different kind, or species, of elephant in each place.

Elephants in Africa

Once there were elephants in all of Africa

south of the Sahara. Today elephants live in only thirty-seven of Africa's fifty-four countries, as far north as Mali and as far south as the nation of South Africa. Elephant habitats, or the places they can safely live, have shrunk in half over the last forty years.

You can tell an African elephant by its flapping ears—they are shaped a little like the continent of Africa itself. And if you get close enough to peer at its trunk, you'll see that the African elephant has two flexible parts on the end. It can use these just like you use a finger and a thumb—to pick up something small.

African savanna elephants are the biggest elephants around. They're also called bush elephants, and they can be ten or even thirteen feet tall at the shoulder, and their heads are higher still! The biggest ones weigh around seven tons.

That's about as much as three pickup trucks.

African forest elephants are a little smaller. They weigh about five and a half tons, a little more than two pickup trucks.

Being about the same weight as a *Tyrannosaurus rex* has some advantages for an animal like an elephant. There aren't many predators who want to tackle a seven-ton animal. At a water hole or a lake, other animals make way. If the elephant spots some leaves at the very

Food that is out of reach for many animals is easy for elephants to grab.

top of a tree that would be out of reach for most? No problem—it can stretch its trunk and snatch those leaves up.

But there is one problem with being so big. Elephants need to eat a *lot*, around 300 pounds of food a day. (If you had an elephant's appetite, you could eat about 330 apples for breakfast, 400 hot dogs for lunch, and 400 plates of spaghetti for dinner—and then do that all again the next day.) Eating is pretty much an elephant's full-time job. It can spend sixteen hours a day munching food.

So the right habitat for an elephant must have a lot of food available. What kind of food? Plants. Elephants are herbivores. They do not eat meat.

To get enough food, elephants need to live somewhere warm where plants can grow all year round. The best habitat for an elephant is around ninety-five degrees Fahrenheit most of the time.

An African forest elephant spends its time in rain forests, eating leaves, fruits, seeds, branches, and bark. The forest trees and bushes provide all the food that this elephant needs.

An African savanna elephant eats grass, leaves, bark, and sometimes even trees that aren't too big. They'll eat fruit, flowers, and nuts as well. These elephants may live in forests, and they can also be found in deserts. (Even in a desert, elephants can find enough food. Desert elephants often prefer to eat grass during the rainy season and trees when it's dry.)

Many savanna elephants live on wide, grassy plains called—you guessed it—savannas. There they wander, sometimes for hundreds of miles a year, eating as they go.

Elephants in Asia

Asian elephants are about the size of African forest elephants. They can grow to be ten feet tall at the shoulder and weigh about five and a half tons.

An Asian elephant's ears are smaller and rounder than an African elephant's. Its back is rounded too, rising in a curve between the

These Asian elephants have smaller ears than their African relatives.

front legs and the back ones. And its trunk has one "finger" on the end instead of two.

Once, Asian elephants lived in an area that reached from the Persian Gulf to the East China Sea. Now they can only be found in parts of India, Nepal, and other nearby countries in Southeast Asia. Their habitat has shrunk to 15 percent of what it used to be.

Wild Asian elephants live in jungles, forests, and grasslands. That's where they can find their food—shrubs, trees, and grass.

Other Asian elephants live with people.

Elephants at Work

African elephants cannot be tamed, but Asian elephants can be. Around a third of Asian elephants are captive. They live with and work for humans.

Companies that cut down trees to harvest wood find elephants very useful. The elephants can go deep into the forest where there are no good roads for trucks or cars. There they can

For centuries, people have used elephants to harvest logs and carry heavy loads. Elephant still do this kind of work for people today.

push down trees and drag or roll logs. The elephants are often used to destroy the very habitats where their ancestors lived.

Other Asian elephants are kept in temples where they take part in ceremonies and festivals or offer blessings to visitors. Long ago, some were trained to carry soldiers into battle. Today, both Asian and African elephants are kept in parks or zoos or circuses where they might do tricks or give rides.

Not every captive elephant is well treated—in fact, many are not. Elephants need a lot of space and a lot of food, more than most owners can give them. It's common for captive elephants to be caged or chained almost all of the time. Trainers sometimes use pointed tools called ankus or bullhooks, hurting the elephants to force them to do what the humans want.

And captive elephants often live by themselves, with no other elephants for company.

In the wild, elephants are born into herds. Female elephants stay with the herd all their lives. Males leave once they are full-grown. Some wander alone for a while. Some find other males to spend time with. Many do a bit of both.

But no wild elephant, male or female, spends its entire life alone. No captive elephant should, either. They need other elephants nearby to feel safe and content.

2

TRUNKS, EARS, AND FAMILIES:
WHAT IT'S LIKE TO BE AN ELEPHANT

Size Is Everything

Like you, an elephant is a mammal—an animal that has fur or hair instead of scales or feathers. An elephant's "fur" is just a few bristles. Babies are hairier than adults. Mammals give birth to babies instead of laying eggs. (Okay, there are two mammals that lay eggs—the echidna and the platypus. They're the exceptions to this rule.) Mammals are also warm-blooded, which means their bodies stay at about the same temperature all the time, no matter how hot or cold the weather gets.

You are similar to an elephant in other ways, too. Like people, most elephants live in family groups where parents take care of children for many years. And elephants live roughly as long as people do—between sixty to seventy years. (The average person lives to be seventy-three.)

But there are differences, too. The biggest difference is, well, big.

Elephants are huge.

So are their noses. An elephant's nose is so big that we call it a trunk. The trunk has tens of thousands of muscles, but not one single bone. It's as flexible as your tongue—it can curl, twist, stretch out long, and scrunch up short.

You use your nose for breathing and smelling

(and maybe to hold up your glasses). An elephant uses its trunk for breathing and smelling too, and for a lot more besides.

An elephant's trunk is as precise as it is strong.

The trunk is strong enough to push down a tree but nimble enough to pick up a single blade of grass. A trunk is useful for making noise, touching other elephants, and picking up anything an elephant wants to stuff into its mouth. Having a trunk is like having a nose that is also a hand, a snorkel, a bulldozer, and a musical instrument.

One thing the trunk *isn't* is a straw. Elephants can't drink through their trunks any more than you can drink through your nose. But they *can* suck water halfway up the trunk. Then they squirt the water right into their mouths—or over their backs for a nice cool shower.

An elephant doesn't just have a big nose—it also has big ears. And those ears are not only for hearing. They are also fans that help cool the elephant off. The hotter the elephant is, the faster the ears flap.

And elephants have big teeth, too. Their

Right: An elephant's trunk doesn't work like a straw—but it is a little like a squirt gun. This Asian elephant is cooling off with a nice spray of water from its trunk.

tusks are extra-long teeth that can be used to dig for food and water, push trees out of the way, or defend the elephant from danger. The tusks keep growing for an elephant's entire life, so the older the elephant, the longer the tusks.

Both male and female African elephants have tusks. Male Asian elephants have tusks, but the females do not.

Besides the tusks, elephants have four teeth inside their mouths—two on the top and two on the bottom. These teeth aren't as big as the tusks, but they aren't small, either. Each is the size of a brick.

Inside your own mouth, you have two sets of teeth—baby teeth that fall out and adult teeth that stay in. But an elephant has six sets. Each set slowly wears out (remember, elephants eat a lot, so they chew a lot) and is replaced by the next. When the sixth set starts to wear out, there is nothing to replace it. So older elephants with worn-down teeth look for food that is easy to chew, like the soft plants that grow in wetlands.

Even an elephant's skin is big—or at least it's thick. It can be up to an inch thick along the animal's back. (In other places, like the ears, it's quite thin.) The skin has many wrinkles and folds that cool the elephant off. The folds trap water, which dries out slowly, helping to keep the animal from getting too warm. It's like wearing a damp shirt on a hot day.

Even thick skin can get sunburned or bitten by insects. Elephants spray water over their skin to protect it, and they may roll in mud or dirt, too. It's like putting on a layer of sunscreen and bug spray all at once.

And finally, an elephant has a big brain, between nine and thirteen pounds. Compare this to our own brains—about three pounds when we are fully grown. This giant brain is useful for gathering in all of the information that comes from the elephant's senses.

What an Elephant Sees, Hears, and Smells

Like you, an elephant has five senses. They hear, see, smell, taste, and touch to find out about the world around them.

An elephant's sense of sight is not particularly strong. That doesn't matter too much, though, because their sense of smell is fantastic.

An elephant has two nostrils that run from one end of the trunk to the other. And its sense of smell is keener than a bloodhound's, which is about a thousand times stronger than a human's. Elephants even have something like an extra nose (it's actually called a vomeronasal organ) on the roof of their mouths to help them smell even better. If an elephant is curious about a particular smell, it might rub its trunk in the new, fascinating aroma and then stick the trunk in its mouth to get the smelly information to its brain.

Elephants can use their sense of smell to find food and water even if it's miles away. They can tell other elephants apart by smell. In one experiment, scientists learned that an elephant can smell which covered bucket had more sunflower seeds in it. Sunflower seeds are a tasty treat for an elephant, and their sensitive noses helped them pick the bucket that would give them more of what they love.

An elephant's big ears also give it a lot of information about what's going on around it. Its sense of hearing is especially useful when it comes to keeping track of other elephants.

A herd of elephants usually stays close together if there's a lot of food nearby. But if food is scarce, the elephants may need to spread out to find enough to eat. If they can't see each other, they can still use their hearing to stay connected.

Elephants make deep rumbling sounds that are too low-pitched for human ears to hear. These sounds can travel for miles. Other elephants hear them or feel the vibrations through their feet or their trunks. Then they know where their herd members are and can join them if they need to.

Touch is another way for elephants to stay

connected with their herd, and they often use their trunks for this. One elephant may put the tip of its trunk in another elephant's mouth as a greeting. Mother elephants use their trunks to pat and stroke their babies. If an elephant seems upset, other elephants sometimes touch it with their trunks.

Staying connected with a herd is very important for an elephant, especially a young one, because a herd is what keeps an elephant safe.

A Herd Is a Family

A baby elephant is called a calf, and they weigh about two hundred pounds when they are born, a bit bigger than the biggest Great Dane. They are three feet tall at birth, so they have a lot of growing to do. And growing, of course, means they have to eat.

All mammal babies (from humans to whales to mice) need milk, either from their mothers or from bottles. Elephant calves drink milk several times a day. They have to—they need a lot of energy to keep up with their herds.

A trunk in the mouth may be a greeting or a way to snatch a bit of a grown-up's food. Maybe both!

Calves drink their mother's milk for somewhere between two to six years. And they also experiment with other kinds of food. A young calf will start to pick up grass and leaves and munch on them. And it may take a little chewed-up food from an adult's mouth and nibble that.

Elephant calves also eat poop. Since adults may poop up to seventeen times a day, there's plenty for a calf to gobble up.

The dung left by adult elephants still has seeds and plants in it that did not get completely broken down, or digested, inside the adult's stomach. That can be good food for the younger elephants. There is also bacteria in the dung, but it doesn't make the babies sick—it's actually good for them. It goes into their own guts and helps them digest the food they eat.

Calves don't spend all their time eating. They love to play and chase other calves, butting heads and wrestling with their trunks. They also charge at animals like egrets or warthogs

Rough-and-tumble play with brothers, sisters, and cousins helps to makes calves strong—plus, it's fun.

to make them run. This is good practice for when the calf grows up and will need to know how to make another animal back off.

Calves also like to roll and wallow in mud. Sometimes a squirming pile of calves will play in a mudhole together.

Mothers watch over their young ones carefully. A mother might let a calf take a nap in the shade under her belly, or use her trunk to help it up a steep slope. And it's not only the mothers who take care of the babies. Other elephants in the herd will also keep an eye on the calves if the mother is busy finding food or water for herself. Female calves between three and twelve years old, who are no longer babies but are too young to have their own calves, do a lot of this babysitting.

And when danger threatens, the entire herd protects the calves. There is no other animal that will try to eat a grown-up elephant, but a calf could be a tasty meal for a lion, a leopard, a tiger, a hyena, or a crocodile. If an elephant signals alarm by giving a trumpeting cry, all the elephants in a herd form into a circle, facing out with the calves in the middle. It would be a brave predator that tried to get past the giant feet, strong trunks, and sharp tusks of the adult elephants.

Have you ever heard the old story that elephants are afraid of mice? It's just a myth. Elephants don't really mind mice, although it's true that they can get startled by any small animal that zips past their feet. But elephants *are* afraid of another tiny animal—bees! Bees can sting an elephant in the places where its skin is thin and sensitive. If an elephant spots or hears a swarm of bees, it often backs away and may make a rumbling call to warn other elephants of the danger. Sometimes adults even form up in their circle, trying to keep the young inside away from the buzzing insects.

The oldest elephant in the herd is usually

the mother or grandmother of all the others. She is the leader, also called the matriarch. (Say it like this: MAY-tree-ark.) The other elephants follow her as she guides them to food and water and warns them of danger nearby. The older a matriarch gets, the more experience she has in keeping her herd safe—and it shows. Mothers who live in herds with older matriarchs have more calves. And calves who are born into herds with older matriarchs have a better chance of surviving than calves in herds led by younger elephants.

You already know that a female calf will spend her life in the herd where she was born, living with her mother, aunts, sisters, cousins, and maybe her grandmother as well. Once she grows up, she'll add her own daughters to the herd.

Male calves leave the herd when they are about ten or twelve. Now and then a male might return to the herd where he was born, spending some time walking and eating with his female relatives.

But males do not stay in the same herd all their lives. There's a simple reason for this—all the elephants in a herd are a family. A young male needs to find mates outside his own family or his babies will not be healthy. His calves will grow up with their mothers, in their own herds, safe and protected and learning how to be elephants.

Unfortunately, being in a herd is not always enough to protect elephants from the threats they face.

3

A WARMING EARTH AND IVORY:
WHY ELEPHANTS ARE ENDANGERED

A hundred years ago, millions of elephants roamed the forests, jungles, and savannas of Africa and Asia.

Today, there are fewer than 450,000 elephants left.

The International Union for the Conservation of Nature keeps track of animal species all over the world. Their Red List of Threatened Species™ has a category for each animal:

Least Concern: This animal is doing all right. There are enough healthy animals to have enough healthy babies to keep the species going.

Near Threatened: This animal is not in trouble yet, but there are danger signs. It may become Vulnerable, Endangered, or Critically Endangered soon.

Vulnerable: There are not many of this animal left, its numbers are falling, and it can live only in certain small areas. It is at risk for extinction.

Endangered: This animal is at *high risk* for extinction.

Critically Endangered: This animal is at *very high risk* for extinction.

Extinct in the Wild: This animal lives only in captivity. There are no wild ones left.

Extinct: This animal is gone forever.

On the Red List, African savanna elephants

and Asian elephants are Endangered. African forest elephants are Critically Endangered.

Why has the number of elephants gotten so small in the last hundred years? What has happened to put elephants at such a high risk for extinction?

Shrinking Habitat

Remember, big animals like elephants need a lot of food and water. That means they need a lot of space. But that space is getting harder and harder to come by.

Today there are more than seven billion people in the world. All of those people need somewhere to live. Cities and towns are growing bigger and bigger.

People are also taking up more and more land to use as farms to grow food. And we need roads and railroad tracks so that we can move between our cities and towns, and so we can move our food from farms to stores and markets and kitchens.

Every new farm or building or road or railroad track built in elephants' habitats means that elephants and other wild animals have less space to live.

Houses and other buildings take up land where elephants once found grass and bushes and trees to eat. Tall fences and busy roads and railroad tracks can block elephants from reaching water holes or salt licks or spots with good food.

And there are times when the opposite problem happens as well. Instead of keeping elephants from getting to their food, people provide elephants with food. Lots and lots of it.

Elephants love some of the crops that humans plant. A field of oil palm trees or bananas or sugarcane or pineapples looks to an elephant like a marvelous meal.

When an elephant knocks down a fence and eats a crop, both the farmer and the elephant are in trouble. The farmer loses valuable food. And if the farmer tries to drive the elephant away, both might get hurt. The farmer might shoot the elephant, or the elephant might trample the farmer. It's not good for either one.

Even if an elephant doesn't make a meal out of a farmer's crops, it might decide that a human trash pile or a garbage dump looks like a tasty treat. But eating human trash can make an elephant sick.

Warmer, Warmer, Warmer

Earth is surrounded by an atmosphere wrapped

around the planet like a blanket. That atmosphere is made up of gases, mostly nitrogen and oxygen.

When sunlight enters Earth's atmosphere, some of it hits the planet and bounces back into space. But not all. Some sunlight is trapped by the atmosphere and stays there, warming up the planet. It's called the greenhouse effect.

The greenhouse effect is part of what makes life possible on Earth. Without it, Earth would be as cold as Mars—about eighty-one degrees below zero. But ever since human beings began to burn coal and oil and gasoline for warmth and energy, we have been putting gases into our atmosphere that trap more of that sunlight.

We call these sources of energy fossil fuels because they are made from fossils, which are the remains of ancient plant and animal life on Earth. The use of fossil fuels is causing the Earth to grow slowly but steadily warmer.

2020 was one of the two warmest years ever recorded. (It tied with 2016.) A warming planet causes problems for all life on Earth—including elephants.

You might not think that a warming planet would make things hard for elephants. After all, they already live in some of Earth's hottest places. But although elephants like things warm, they can't get *too* warm. If the weather gets up to 113 degrees, even for short heat waves, elephants can get sick. They can also get sunburned.

A warming climate changes how and where plants grow. If it becomes too hot for certain plants, elephants can lose the food that's best for them to eat.

Like all living things (including zebras), elephants need water to survive. A warming world means it's harder for them to find the water they need.

And a warming world means it's hard for elephants to find water. An elephant can drink more than fifty gallons a day, and they also need water to swim and bathe in. They get wet not just for fun, but also to keep themselves from overheating.

As the planet warms, there are more droughts—times with little or no rain. Lakes and rivers and water holes dry up. Plants that elephants eat wither and die.

Elephants who can't get enough to eat or drink may die as well. If they survive, they will be weaker and less healthy. Weaker elephants may not have babies at all, or they may give birth to calves that are not strong themselves. Weaker calves have less of a chance of growing up to have calves of their own.

And elephants aren't the only ones who need water, of course. Other wild animals need it and so do people. People need water to drink, to give to their own animals (like cows and sheep and goats), and to keep their crops alive.

If water gets scarce, people may start taking

it from places where elephants drink. Or elephants may come closer and closer to farms and houses, looking for water. It's not safe for people or for elephants if they get their water from the same places.

If people take action now, we may be able to save elephants from the effects of a warming world. And elephants might be able to return the favor.

As scientists studied African forest elephants, they realized that these elephants are actually changing the forests they live in—and they are changing it in a way that helps to fight global warming.

Forest elephants like to eat vines, leaves, bark, and smaller branches of trees. They're sloppy eaters, too. They trample trees, tear down vines, and basically make a mess.

Just by finding the food they need, these African forest elephants are helping to protect the world from climate change.

They tend to knock down softwood trees that are less than one foot thick. "Softwood" means just what it sounds like—the wood from these kinds of trees is soft and easy for elephants to chew.

So as elephants move through the forest, they take down smaller softwood trees and leave the larger hardwood trees alone. (You guessed it—"hardwood" means just what it sounds like, too—trees that have tougher, stronger wood.) Then the bigger trees have more room to grow. It's easier for sunlight to reach them. So they just keep on getting bigger.

Over time, forests where elephants live have more bigger hardwood trees and fewer smaller softwood trees. And that's important, because trees (and other plants) take a gas called carbon dioxide into their leaves. Their leaves also give out oxygen.

Oxygen is what humans (and elephants and other animals) need to breathe. We'd die without it. And carbon dioxide is one of the gases that helps trap heat in the atmosphere. It makes global warming worse.

The small trees that the elephants knock

over take in small amounts of carbon dioxide. But the big ones that the elephants leave standing? They soak up a *lot* of carbon dioxide.

By making the forest a better place for big trees, forest elephants are helping to fight global warming. If humans can do the same thing, it will be good for the elephants and for us.

Hunting for Ivory

The third serious threat to elephants comes from the only predator who can hunt and kill a full-grown elephant—a human being.

People sometimes hunt elephants for their meat. They might even make an elephant's skin into jewelry or a kind of medicine. (Some people believe that elephant skin can cure skin diseases or clear up pimples. It can't.) Elephant feet have even been made into furniture! But the most common reason elephants are killed is for their tusks.

When a tusk is taken, cut, carved, and polished, it becomes something that humans have

Tusks like these, taken from elephants . . .

loved and prized for centuries: ivory. The word "elephant" actually comes from a Greek word, "elephas," which means "ivory."

Ivory can come from the tusks of animals other than elephants. Hippos, walruses, sperm whales, narwhals, and some warthogs or wild boars also have tusks or teeth that can be made into ivory.

... can be turned into art like this carved ivory bracelet, made by a sculptor of the Yoruba people of West Africa.

But the ivory made from elephant tusks is thought to be more beautiful than the ivory made from the teeth of any other animal. And elephant tusks are huge. Killing one elephant will get you much more ivory than killing one warthog or narwhal or walrus. A single tusk from an African elephant can reach six feet—that's probably longer than your teacher is tall. It can weigh fifty pounds, as much as an average seven-year-old kid.

For centuries, people have made tusks into ivory because it's so lovely to look at and because it can be carved into almost any shape. We have used it to make jewelry, piano keys, fans, pool balls, furniture, and even false teeth. People want ivory not just because they like how it looks, but because it's rare and expensive. Owning something made of ivory makes people feel rich and important.

Ivory is so valuable that people sometimes call it "white gold." In 2014, people would pay

$2,100 for 2.2 pounds of ivory. (The price has gone down a little since then, but ivory is still worth a lot of money.)

In Africa today, one elephant is killed about every fifteen minutes, usually to take its tusks and make them into ivory. The rest of the elephant is often left to rot.

Killing one elephant is bad enough, but it is not always the end of the story. Hunters naturally go after the elephants with the biggest tusks they can find. This means they kill the largest and oldest males, and then the largest and oldest females. These old females are likely to be matriarchs, the mothers of many calves and the leaders of their herds.

If a mother with a calf dies, the calf isn't likely to live. If the leader of a herd is killed, her herd may be in trouble. And if an old male is slaughtered, he will have no more calves who might grow up to have their own babies one day.

So killing a single elephant for its tusks can lead to many fewer elephants in the world. If people keep on hunting elephants at the rate we are now, there may be none left in the wild in a few hundred years.

Today, we don't have to make piano keys or pool balls or false teeth out of ivory. We can make them out of wood or plastic or other materials. There is simply no need to kill elephants for ivory.

Thankfully, more and more people are starting to understand this.

4

RULE MAKERS, RESEARCHERS, FILMMAKERS, RANGERS, AND BEES: WHO HAS BEEN SAVING ELEPHANTS?

Saving elephants in the wild means making sure they have what they need: food, water, enough space to roam, and safety from hunters who want to kill them for their tusks, meat, or skin.

There are people all over the world trying to make sure elephants can get all of these things.

No More Selling Ivory

Some of the people helping elephants may never even have seen one. They do not trek through the jungles of Asia or the savannas of Africa looking for elephants to help.

Instead they write laws and make rules to keep elephants and other animals safe.

One of the most important of these rules is a treaty with a very long name. It's called the Convention on International Trade in Endangered Species of Wild Fauna and Flora. ("Fauna" means animals, "flora" means plants, and a treaty is a set of rules that different countries agree to follow.) The whole thing is called CITES for short.

One hundred and eighty-three countries (including the United States) have agreed to follow the rules set out in CITES. Those rules govern whether people can buy and sell endangered animals and plants or things that are made from them—everything from tiger skins to the wood of the mahogany tree to jewelry carved from coral.

Before 1989, CITES had no rules about elephants. It was completely legal to kill elephants for their tusks and sell the ivory. So of course that's what people did. Between 1979 and 1989, Africa lost half of its wild elephants, many of them killed for their tusks.

In 1989, that changed. Elephants were added to the list of protected animals in CITES. This meant there were very strict rules about buying and seling ivory in the countries who agreed to follow the CITES rules.

This didn't stop the trade in ivory completely. Not every country has signed on to

CITES. And in countries that did, many people broke (and still break) the rules, secretly killing elephants for their tusks. This kind of illegal hunting is called poaching, and it continues to be a serious threat to elephants.

Still, the ban on ivory trading did help protect a lot of elephants. Of course, a rule is only as good as the people who make sure the rule is followed.

Safe Spaces

One of the most important things that elephants need is space. One of the best ways to give them that space is to create parks and conservation areas where no building or hunting is allowed.

These parks have rules to protect elephants and other animals, but the rules don't do much good unless someone is there to make sure people obey them. That's what park rangers do.

One such park, Zakouma National Park in Chad, had lost thousands of its elephants to poachers. By 2010, only four hundred were left. People predicted that in a few years there would be no elephants in the park at all.

That didn't happen. The park hired more rangers to protect the elephants, provided more training for them, and made sure that there were enough of them to work all year round. Now the rangers could do a better job of protecting the elephants. In 2011, only six elephants in Zakouma were killed by poachers. In 2014, fifty new calves were born. In 2017, there were seventy.

The elephant population in Zakouma started

*A ranger at the Sheldrick Wildlife Trust
cares for an orphaned elephant calf.*

to grow again because of everything the park
rangers did to protect the elephants.

And the elephants returned the favor.
Tourists come to parks like Zakouma eager to
see elephants and other wildlife. That means
park rangers, guides, and people who work at
nearby hotels and restaurants can earn money

that they and their families need. The people help the elephants, and the elephants help the people.

That's the case at parks and conservation areas all over Africa and Asia, including Amboseli National Park on the border between Kenya and Tanzania. There a protector of elephants has been at work for more than fifty years.

Studying and Saving Elephants

While Cynthia Moss was growing up, she did not know that science would become her life's work. But as a teenager, when she rode her horse through the forests of New York state, she felt completely happy to be surrounded by nature. Those trail rides were the beginnings of a life dedicated to animals.

Moss moved to New York City in 1964 to become a reporter. She might have spent her life there if a friend had not invited her to visit East Africa. While she was there, Moss met a scientist doing research on elephants in Tanzania who offered her a job as his assistant. She returned to New York just long enough to give up her apartment and make plans for the move. In 1968, she began studying elephants in earnest. When the project wrapped up later that year, Moss found other jobs—working as a veterinarian's assistant and writing a report for a film company—so that she could stay.

In 1972, Moss arrived at Amboseli National Park, ready to learn more about the elephants there.

Amboseli has hundreds of elephants and enough space for them to live. It has enough water, too. Snow on nearby Mount Kilimanjaro melts and flows into swamps in the park, holding enough water to support elephants and other animals as well. Zebras, giraffes, hyenas, antelopes, hippos, and lions all make their homes in Amboseli.

Moss set up a simple camp where she and other scientists could live in tents while they worked. For many years, there was not even a telephone there. Moss believed that distractions and interruptions from the outside world would make it harder to focus on the work that needed to be done.

One of Moss's first jobs as a scientist was to observe and photograph all of Amboseli's elephants so that she could come to know each one. Every elephant was given a name. Usually all of the elephants in one family group would

Cynthia Moss's work in Amboseli National Park changed how people think of elephants.

have names that started with the same letter. In one group, for example, a mother named Echo had calves named Ely, Enid, Eliot, and Ebony.

Moss and the other scientists who have worked with her have followed and studied the same elephants for decades. Every year they learn more about how elephants live, how they think, how they interact with each other, how they make their way around the park, and much more besides. They have put radio collars on elephants to track how far and where the elephants travel. They have studied the ways that elephants communicate with both sounds and body language. They've traced the many relationships between family groups.

Moss's work helped many people all over the world come to see elephants as fascinating, intelligent creatures with deep ties to one another. The discoveries made at Amboseli about how elephants live have shown the best ways to keep wild elephants safe and have also made life better for captive elephants all over the world.

Learning about elephants was not enough for Cynthia Moss. She desperately wants to share her knowledge with others, so she makes it a point to give interviews and offer tours of

Amboseli to writers and reporters. She has written several books (two of them for children) and helped make four documentary movies about elephants.

In 2001, she started the Amboseli Trust for Elephants. The goal of the trust is to keep the elephants of Amboseli safe and to create a better world for elephants everywhere.

One thing that the Trust tries to do is to help people and elephants live peacefully together. Many people of the Maasai tribe live near Amboseli, and sometimes the cows, goats, and sheep that the Maasai raise for meat and milk are in danger from elephants. (An elephant will not kill another animal to eat it; remember, they only eat plants. But it may hurt or trample another animal if it feels threatened or if the animal is simply in its way.)

If an elephant kills an animal that belongs to one of the Maasai people, Maasai hunters would traditionally try to kill that elephant. The Amboseli Trust instead began offering to pay a fee for any animal that an elephant killed. After the Trust began paying, the number of elephants killed in revenge dropped by half.

Protecting elephants who live in the wild—like the ones in Amboseli—is something we absolutely must do if elephants are to survive. But not all elephants are wild—and elephants who live with and work for people need protection, too.

In Temples, in Chains

When Sangita Iyer was a child, living in the Indian state of Kerala, her grandfather would take her to visit a nearby temple. She loved to see the elephant that lived there. All over India—and especially in Kerala—people throng to temples to see elephants who touch worshippers with their trunks to offer them a blessing. During big festivals, temple elephants are often decorated and marched through crowded streets.

When Iyer grew up, she became a journalist and a filmmaker and made her home in Toronto, Canada. Returning to Kerala on a visit, she realized that the elephants she'd loved seeing as a child were often mistreated in horrifying ways. Chained for hours and hours, they had painful wounds on their legs. They were often savagely beaten by trainers called mahouts, who believed it was the only way to make such big animals obey their commands. She met one temple elephant with an injured

Worshippers and tourists are drawn to temples by the elephants who are kept there—but many don't realize how badly these elephants may be treated.

eye oozing tears, and another with a trunk that was partly paralyzed. This elephant could not even use his trunk to bring water to his mouth.

Iyer returned to Kerala with a film crew, and they recorded more than twenty-five hours of video showing how the temple elephants were treated. She also interviewed scientists, priests, and experts in animal welfare, all calling for change. After three years of work, Iyer completed a film called *Gods in Shackles*. It revealed just how much the elephants were suffering while they patiently touched visitor after visitor with their trunks or marched through crowded, noisy streets.

The film was shown all over the world and won several awards. Iyer hopes it will open people's eyes to the suffering of Kerala's temple elephants and encourage lawmakers to create new rules to protect them.

Rules and laws are one way to protect elephants, both the wild ones and the ones who live with people. Another strategy is to get some help from bees.

Yes, bees.

Good Fences Make Good Neighbors

Remember that elephants don't like bees? People have used this fact to keep elephants away from farms and crops.

It's hard to make a fence tall and strong enough to keep out an elephant who is determined to raid a field full of juicy pineapples or sweet sugarcane. But one thing that does work is a beehive fence.

Farmers can surround a field with tall wooden posts. Wires are strung from the posts, and beehives are hung from the wires. If an elephant pushes against the wire, the beehive sways, and the bees swarm out to protect their home. The elephant usually decides to go elsewhere to look for food—somewhere it won't be bothered by bees. And that's safer for the crops, the farmers, and the elephants as well.

Park rangers and scientists and filmmakers, people making rules about the ivory trade or choices about buying and selling ivory, bees just trying to keep their hives safe—there are many people (and some animals) helping elephants. No one wants to live in a world without elephants. If we keep working together, we can make sure that we don't have to.

SOME FUN FACTS ABOUT ELEPHANTS

1. Elephants can only sweat on their toes. Since the places they live are hot pretty much all the time, elephants cool off by swimming and spraying themselves with water.

2. Female Asian elephants don't grow true tusks. Sometimes, though, their incisor teeth (the pointy ones at the sides of the mouth) do grow long enough to poke out of their mouths. These long teeth are called "tushes." Some females have them and some don't.

3. Elephants walk on tiptoe. Their toes are at the front of their feet. On the back, what we would think of as the heel, is actually a thick pad of fat that helps to cushion their heavy weight.

4. Baby elephants sometimes suck their own trunks, very much like human babies suck their thumbs.

5. The largest elephant ever recorded was an adult male African savanna elephant who weighed twenty-four thousand pounds and was thirteen feet tall at the shoulder.

6. The elephant's closest living relatives are manatees and dugongs (these aquatic mammals are sometimes called "sea cows") and the hyrax, which is a rodent that looks a bit like a prairie dog.

7. Elephants have some extinct relatives as well. Mammoths and mastodons, which roamed the earth in prehistoric times, looked a lot like hairy elephants.

8. Elephants can't jump.

9. Each elephant has a preferred tusk—left or right—that they use more often, just as a person might be left- or right-handed.

10. Elephants can be identified by their ears. No two elephants have ears that are exactly alike.

11. An elephant is pregnant with a calf for twenty-two months, more than twice as long as a human.

HOW YOU CAN HELP SAVE THE ELEPHANTS

Who would want to live in a world without elephants? We can all try to make our planet a better place for endangered or vulnerable species. Here are some things that you can do to help:

1. Don't buy jewelry or anything made of ivory. (Maybe someone you know has a piece of ivory that they or their family have owned for many years. This is okay—some ivory was made, bought, and sold before today's rules were made.) But don't buy new ivory!

2. Maybe you're thinking, "I'm just a kid—how would I buy any ivory anyway?" It's true that ivory is expensive. But you can still use your words and your knowledge to explain to others that it's important not to buy or sell ivory. If no one is buying ivory, no elephants will be killed for their tusks.

3. Support parks and reserves and sanctuaries where elephants can be protected. You can't make an elephant park in your own backyard, but you could hold a bake sale or do chores around the house or your neighborhood to raise money for places like the Amboseli Trust for Elephants in Kenya or the Elephant Nature Park in Thailand or Wildlife SOS in India or the Sheldrick Wildlife Trust in Kenya.

4. Get some other kids to help. If your whole class holds a bake sale, or you get several friends together to mow lawns, rake leaves, or have a lemonade stand, you'll make more money to donate!

5. Do your part to reduce global warming. Every bit helps. Avoid using fossil fuels when you can. That might mean riding your bike to a friend's house (if you can) instead of asking for a ride or encouraging your parents to turn down the heat a little in winter and wearing a warm sweater.

6. Recycling is also good. Every can or plastic bottle that gets recycled means less energy was used to make a new one. And that means fewer fossil fuels were burned.

7. Reusing is even better than recycling! Instead of drinking from a plastic water bottle and recycling it, bring your own bottle to be filled up over and over again.

8. Don't go to circuses or shows that have elephants do tricks or give rides. Elephants in these kinds of places are rarely treated well.

9. If there are elephants at your local zoo, check out their habitat. Is it big enough that the elephants can move around? Is there just one elephant, or is there a group or at least a pair for company? Do the elephants have enough to do? A good zoo will give elephants interesting things to look at (maybe mirrors), smell (perfume or spices are nice),

touch (some elephants like the feel of rubber tires), play with (logs or barrels can be fun), and, of course, eat. If the elephants don't seem well treated, you can write to the zoo asking for changes.

10. Write to the politicians who represent your city, state, and country asking them to take global warming seriously. You can't vote yet—but one day you will. And that means leaders care about what you and kids like you think. You can go to USA.gov/Elected-Officials to find out who your representatives are and how to contact them.

11. Learn more about elephants. You can check out some of these books:

5 Elephants
by Rob Laidlaw

How to Be an Elephant
by Katherine Roy

Elephant Woman: Cynthia Moss
Explores the World of Elephants
by Laurence Pringle

Little Big Ears: The Story of Ely
by Cynthia Moss

12. Tell your friends and family some of the things you've learned. Elephants are amazing animals. If others know more about them, they will want to protect them, too.

REFERENCES

"African Elephant." National Geographic. Accessed October 1, 2020. nationalgeographic.com/animals /mammals/a/african-elephant.

"African Elephants and Climate Change." World Wildlife Fund. Accessed June 16, 2021. worldwildlife.org/pages /african-elephants-and-climate-change--3.

Amboseli Trust for Elephants. Accessed June 18, 2021. elephanttrust.org/index.php.

Angier, Natalie. "What Has Four Legs, a Trunk and a Behavioral Database?" *The*

New York Times, June 4, 2021.

nytimes.com/2021/06/04/science
/african-elephants-ethogram-behavior
-poole.html.

"Asian Elephants and Climate Change."
World Wildlife Fund. Accessed June 16,
2021. worldwildlife.org/pages/asian
elephants-and-climate-change.

"Battles Over Ever Decreasing Land." World
Wildlife Fund. Accessed June 23, 2021.
wwf.panda.org/discover/knowledge_hub
/endangered_species/elephants
/human_elephant_conflict.

"Diet and Eating Habits." SeaWorld Parks &
Entertainment. Accessed June 21, 2021.
https://seaworld.org/animals/all-about
/elephants/diet.

Eaton, Maxwell III. *The Truth About Elephants.* New York: Roaring Brook Press, 2018.

"Elephant." African Wildlife Foundation. Accessed October 1, 2020. awf.org /wildlife-conservation/elephant.

"Elephant." San Diego Zoo Wildlife Alliance, Animals and Plants. Accessed October 2, 2020. animals.sandiegozoo.org /animals/elephant.

"Gentle Giants." Anamalai: India's Elephant Mountain. PBS. Accessed June 22, 2021. pbs.org/edens/anamalai/gentle.html.

"Gods in Shackles: Plight of Temple Elephants." *The Times of India.* July 20, 2016. timesofindia.indiatimes.com/city/chennai /Gods-in-shackles-Plight-of-temple-elephants/articleshow/53298377.cms.

Haines, Gavin. "New Documentary Exposes Brutal Treatment of India's Temple Elephants." *The Telegraph*. July 5, 2016. telegraph.co.uk/travel/destinations/asia/india/articles/new-documentary-exposes-abuse-of-indias-sacred-elephants.

"Ivory." Encyclopaedia Britannica Online. Accessed June 10, 2021. britannica.com/topic/ivory.

Laidlaw, Rob. *5 Elephants*. Markham, ON: Fitzhenry & Whiteside, 2017.

Mumby, Hannah. *Elephants: Birth, Life, and Death in the World of the Giants*. New York: HarperCollins, 2020.

Natarajan, Swaminathan. "The Woman Trying to Save India's Tortured Temple Elephants." BBC. September 7, 2020. bbc.com/news/world-asia-india-54026294.

Nuwer, Rachel. "The Thick Gray Line:
  Forest Elephants Defend Against Climate
  Change." *The New York Times,* August 19,
  2019. nytimes.com/2019/08/19/science
  /elephants-climate-change.html.

Pinnock, Don, and Colin Bell, eds. *The Last
  Elephants.* Washington, DC: Smithsonian
  Books, 2019.

Pringle, Laurence. *Elephant Woman: Cynthia
  Moss Explores the World of Elephants.*
  Photographs by Cynthia Moss. New York:
  Atheneum Books, 1997.

Roy, Katherine. *How to Be an Elephant:
  Growing Up in the African Wild.* New York:
  Roaring Brook Press. 2017.

SARAH L. THOMSON has published more than thirty books, including prose and poetry, fiction and non-fiction, picture books and novels. Her work includes two adventures featuring a teenage girl ninja, a riveting survival story about wildfires and wombats, and non-fiction about elephants, sharks, tigers, plesiosaurs, saber-toothed cats, and other fascinating creatures.

School Library Journal called Sarah's picture book *Cub's Big World* "a big must-have." The *Bulletin of the Center for Children's Books* described her novel *Deadly Flowers* as "clever, dangerous, vivacious," and *Booklist* said this fantasy set in feudal Japan is "genuinely thrilling, with surprises at every turn and a solid emotional core." *Deadly Flowers* also received Wisconsin's Elizabeth Burr/Worzalla Award.

Sarah worked as an editor at HarperCollins and Simon & Schuster before becoming a full-time writer. She lives in Portland, Maine.

Photo courtesy of the author

Learn more about her work at
SarahLThomson.com

CHELSEA CLINTON is the author of the #1 *New York Times* best-seller *She Persisted: 13 American Women Who Changed the World*; *She Persisted Around the World: 13 Women Who Changed History*; *She Persisted in Sports: American Olympians Who Changed the Game*; *Don't Let Them Disappear: 12 Endangered Species Across the Globe*; *It's Your World: Get Informed, Get Inspired & Get Going!*; *Start Now!: You Can Make a Difference*; with Hillary Clinton, *Grandma's Gardens* and *The Book of Gutsy Women: Favorite Stories of Courage and Resilience*; and, with Devi Sridhar, *Governing Global Health: Who Runs the World and Why?* She is also the Vice Chair of the Clinton Foundation, where she works on many initiatives, including those that help empower the next generation of leaders. She lives in New York City with her husband, Marc, their children and their dog, Soren.

Photo courtesy of the author

You can follow Chelsea Clinton on Twitter
@ChelseaClinton
or on Facebook at
Facebook.com/ChelseaClinton

DON'T MISS MORE BOOKS IN THE

save the . . .
BLUE WHALES
Christine Taylor-Butler
With an introduction by Chelsea Clinton

save the . . .
ELEPHANTS
Sarah L. Thomson
With an introduction by Chelsea Clinton

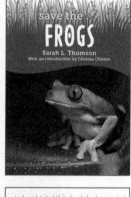

save the . . .
FROGS
Sarah L. Thomson
With an introduction by Chelsea Clinton

save the . . .
LIONS
Sarah L. Thomson
With an introduction by Chelsea Clinton

save the . . .
POLAR BEARS
Christine Taylor-Butler
With an introduction by Chelsea Clinton

save the . . . SERIES!

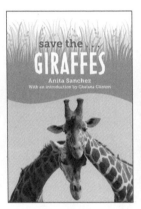

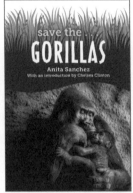

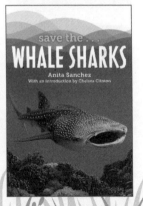